MAKING TV WORK FOR YOUR FAMILY

MAKING TV WORK FOR YOUR FAMILY

William L. Coleman

BETHANY HOUSE PUBLISHERS
MINNEAPOLIS, MINNESOTA 55438
A Division of Bethany Fellowship, Inc.

Photos by Dick Easterday and Larry Swenson

Scripture verses marked KJV are taken from the King James Version of
the Bible. Verses marked TLB are taken from The Living Bible,
copyright © 1971 by Tyndale House Publishers, Wheaton, Ill. Used by
permission.

Published by Bethany House Publishers
A Division of Bethany Fellowship, Inc.
6820 Auto Club Road, Minneapolis, MN 55438

Printed in the United States of America

Library of Congress Cataloging in Publication Data

Coleman, William L.
    Making TV work for your family.

    1. Family—United States. 2. Television programs—United States.
I. Title. II. Title: Making TV work for your family.
HQ536.C7   1983   306.8'5   83-11881
ISBN 0-87123-322-3

WILLIAM L. COLEMAN is becoming increasingly well known as a gifted writer and author. His specialty has been devotional books for families, which have become bestsellers.

Coleman is a graduate of the Washington Bible College in Washington, D.C., and Grace Theological Seminary in Winona Lake, Indiana. He has pastored churches and is presently a full-time writer. His articles have appeared in several well-known evangelical magazines. Bill, his wife and three children make their home in Aurora, Nebraska.

Other Books
by William Coleman
from Bethany House Publishers

Contents

Enjoy Television

Our television set is one of the most interesting things in our home. It can provide entertainment and good education. Sometimes it makes us laugh. Sometimes it makes us concerned. At other times television teaches us how fast an ostrich can run in the rain.

If you want to make the best use of your television, you must learn to control your viewing time and choose what you watch. I hope this book will help you and your family decide how to use your television in a great way.

Bill Coleman
Aurora, Nebraska

How to Use This Book

This book is written in such a way that it could easily be read to the family by one of the children. We suggest reading a chapter once a week and allowing each family member to answer the questions at the end on a separate piece of paper. Afterward, each one could read his/her answers, and an interesting discussion could follow. After your discussion it would be a good idea to pray together as a family. Besides praying for each other, your church and your missionaries, pray that God will show your family how to use TV in the best possible way.

1 | The Age of Television

Watching television can be a great deal of fun. Television is interesting, entertaining and educational. Sometimes it is exciting, happy, sad or just a good way to spend an hour.

There are few things as popular in the United States as the television set. Almost everyone has one. Some people do not have a bathtub but they have a television set. Some children do not have a refrigerator in their home but they have a TV.

Your children and your grandchildren will probably grow up watching a set. If television is going to be around for a long time, we need to know more about this electronic system and how to use it well. Television well-used can be a wonderful part of our lives. But like everything else, if TV is used poorly, it can be harmful.

Practically everyone around us watches television. You might know someone who doesn't have one; however, over half the households in the U.S. have two television sets or more.

Television is becoming a large business with many

different possibilities. There are channels that show only sports or news or religious programs.

Many families are buying video cassette recorders so they can tape shows and play them later. Thousands of children have television games that allow them to play Ping-Pong or blow up spaceships on the screen. You can even buy a special chair to sit in for playing video games!

Some families own sets they play inside their cars or portable ones to take on picnics or boats. A certain electronics company is making a tiny set that you can wear like a wristwatch.

The future of TV is difficult to guess. Television sets will probably be connected to computers. The average viewer will gather information, get help with his homework, read a book on the screen or do many other things—without leaving his chair!

Television phones are already available in some places. By pushing a button the caller can *see* the person he or she is talking to.

As you discuss the subject, your opinions and suggestions are important. Naturally, mothers and fathers set the final guidelines, but they need to hear from you.

1. How many television sets do you have in your home?
2. What rooms are your television sets in?
3. How many are black and white? How many are color?
4. Would you like another set? Why?
5. How many channels can your set receive?
6. Do you have cable TV?
7. Do you subscribe to Home Box Office (HBO)?
8. Do you have a video cassette recorder?
9. Is your television a floor model or a portable set?
10. Do you enjoy watching television? Why?
11. Do your parents enjoy watching television? Why?

Television, like every other object in this world, is not good or bad. The way it is *used* makes it good or bad.

"I know, and am persuaded by the Lord Jesus, that there is nothing unclean of itself" (Rom. 14:14, KJV).

2 | Why Is Television Good?

Apples are good, but if apples are all we eat, we will soon become sick. Running is excellent for our health, but if we run day and night we will quickly collapse.

Children and parents both know that television offers many good things. Each of us has watched a program and afterward said, "That was great!" or "I wish they would put on more shows like that."

Some studies have been made which suggest that children often treat each other kindly if they have watched a kind person on television. This is called pro-social behavior. The same thing can happen when we see parents, brothers and sisters or friends being nice to each other.

Television is not all good. Later we will discuss some problems which result from watching it. However, we also need to emphasize its strong points.

Many of us are more aware of hunger and poverty in the world because we watch television. Sometimes we have the courage to help others partly because we saw a person do it on our favorite show. More than once we have seen an excellent Christian program and learned more about God.

There are many reasons why television is good. You probably have a few reasons of your own. Your opinion is important. It is great if your parents know how you feel. It is also helpful if you know what they are thinking.

1. What is your favorite show?
2. Why do you like it?
3. Who is the leading person in your show?
4. Describe this person.
5. What kind of good things do people do on this show?
6. Does this show make you want to do better? Explain.
7. In your opinion, what are some of the good things that come from watching television?
8. Make a list of your favorite shows. Next to each one write one good thing about the show.
9. In your opinion, is there more good on television than bad?
10. What is your parents' favorite show?
11. Why do they like it?

If you listed some good things that come from television, you can praise God for your set. Television can be used to help you and your parents.

"But whatever is good and perfect comes to us from God, the Creator of all light, and he shines forever without change or shadow" (James 1:17, TLB).

3 | Looking for Heroes

Heroes have always been important. They are the people we look up to, respect, and often want to be like. A hero isn't someone who is perfect but someone brave, strong, wise, intelligent or something else good.

Children aren't the only ones who have heroes. Many adults greatly admire a senator, a soldier, a judge or a kind mechanic who lives nearby. Heroes are often helpful because their example makes us want to do better.

A good hero doesn't have to be real. You might have a hero in a comic book or in cartoons or your hero could be mythical. Sometimes our heroes are historical characters like Daniel Boone, Abraham Lincoln, the astronauts or Amelia Earhart, the pilot. Their good accomplishments usually mean more to us than whether they are real, pretend, living or dead.

Most of us are willing to accept a hero who isn't perfect. That's part of growing up. One day we learn that our favorite cowboy has a terrible drug habit. We find out that a singer we like has been in jail. We discover that a seemingly patient television star lost his temper and said some terrible things.

Our hero doesn't have to be perfect. We aren't perfect, either, so we can accept that. Only Jesus Christ is perfect.

Television has a few excellent heroes. They aren't perfect, but they're very good. Some of them risk their lives to help others. Some are kind and thoughtful to children. Others are intelligent and solve problems to help thousands of people. A few heroes show love and gentleness, and that makes us feel good and want to do the same thing.

Your hero might be a Muppet with green fuzzy hair. Your hero could be a pretend visitor from another planet. It could be a policeman on television, an athlete, a doctor, or a taxicab driver.

The Bible is filled with heroes. Those stories and their characters make us want to do our best.

Unfortunately some people pick out a terrible hero. The decide they want to be like a crook or a cheater or a drunk or a cruel person.

It's important to pick out the right kind of hero. He will influence the way you think.

There are some terrific heroes on television. If you choose them carefully, they can help you want to be a better person.

Good heroes make good examples for us to follow.

"I have given you an example to follow: do as I have done to you" [Jesus] (John 13:15, TLB).

1. Name three people or characters that you feel make good heroes on television.
2. Why do you like these heroes?
3. Explain one thing you do not like about one of your television heroes.
4. Name two television characters whom you think make poor or bad heroes for us to follow.

5. Explain what makes them poor choices.
6. How many of your television heroes are: a) women, b) men, c) children, d) animals, e) Muppets, f) cartoon characters, or g) athletes?
7. Name three of your favorite Bible heroes.
8. If you could decide, what kind of heroes would you like to see more of on television?

4 | Surprise!

If you watch television a great deal of the time, you might be in for some big surprises. The real world we live in is much different than the one we watch on our set.

On soap operas it looks like every day is terrible. The characters seem sad most of the time and each day brings a new tragedy. They appear to always be in trouble.

Life has plenty of trouble but it also has loads of happiness. If we believe what we see on soap operas, life looks like one big headache.

Another big surprise is how many wealthy people are on television. Most characters seem to have huge new homes, large new cars, and they often fly places. They also have a great many expensive, stylish clothes. Several homes have butlers, maids and chauffeur-driven cars.

There are people who live this way, but very few. I have *never* been to a home where a butler opened the door.

When we watch this level of living, we sometimes think we must become rich, too. The fact is that most of us will never be rich and some people don't even want to be rich. Life is a lot different than television.

It seems like there are a great many lawyers and doctors on television. Another big surprise. There are far more mechanics, bus drivers, real estate salesmen, truck drivers, insurance salesmen and carpenters than television would lead us to believe.

Lawyers and doctors can be great people, but millions of others are just as happy with their jobs.

If you watch a lot of television, the world might look more dangerous than it really is. There is plenty of real danger in life, but not as much as television presents.

It might be a big surprise to you, but I have never been robbed or mugged. Neither have most of my friends.

There are things to be afraid of in life. All of us should be careful what we do and where we go. However, it is not as dangerous as it looks on television.

Some children (and some adults) are frequently afraid because of what they watch on television.

Here's good news. Life is often much better than television makes it look.

1. Whom do you see on television that looks fairly happy?
2. Why do you think so many people on television look rich?
3. Do you think television makes people jealous and unhappy with what they have? Explain.
4. Does this ever happen to you? If so, when?
5. Do your parents believe television gives a false view of life?
6. Do you think police work is really the way it is on a police show?
7. How do you imagine police work might be different?
8. What do your parents think about police shows?

5 | How Long to Watch It

We are becoming the television generation. The average child spends most of the evening watching his set. Maybe the average adult does, too.

Between the ages of two and eleven, the average child watches television three and one half hours a day, nearly twenty-five hours a week. Often preschool children occupy over four hours of their waking day watching their favorite programs.

It's easy to see what a great influence television has on us. In fact, few other things are as big a part of our lives as the magic tube.

How much time we spend watching TV is only part of the question. We also must ask ourselves if we are neglecting other important things while we are fixed in front of the set. Do our studies suffer; are we forgetting to help around the house; are we giving up reading; do we ignore our family, friends and others.

The answers are not the same for everyone. Some people seem to get everything done. However, what might be the right amount of television for one person may be too much for someone else. It is a question you and your family must work out together.

One pattern to watch in your life is *when* you turn off the set. Do you turn it off when you are told to? If you are not told to turn it off, do you watch it for hours whether or not you like the programs?

If you watch it endlessly without caring what is on, television is too big a habit in your life. If you can pick and choose programs and turn it off when you are not interested, you may be moving toward mature, selective television viewing.

When a person picks programs and then turns off the set that person controls his television. If he can't choose, the TV controls him.

Take your own survey of your watching habits and your parents'.

1. *Without counting,* guess how many hours of television you watched last week.
2. Actually count the number of hours you watched television last week and write that number down.
3. Do you think your last week's viewing was too little, too much, or just right? Why?
4. How many hours did your parents watch last week? If your mother's and father's times are different, list them separately.
5. How do your parents feel about the amount of time they spent watching television last week?
6. Take a time check. How much time did you spend doing each of these last week?

Reading	Watching television
Sleeping	Helping around the
Helping others	house
Listening to tapes	Playing indoor games
or records	Playing outdoor games
Eating	Talking to parents
Going to school	Talking to friends

7. What four things did you spend the most time doing?
8. What would you like to spend more time doing?
9. Do you think television usually takes too much of your time, too little, or just right? Explain.
10. Do you think television affects your schoolwork? How?
11. Do your parents think television affects your schoolwork? How?

It is important to answer these questions. It could help you understand yourself by knowing how you spend your time.

"There is a right time for everything" (Eccles. 3:1, TLB).

6 | Enjoying the Sports World

If you enjoy sports, television is a lot of fun because it allows you to see a wide variety of top events. On the same day you can see championship basketball, major league baseball, and soccer from London. Without leaving your living room, you can see close-ups of the best quarterbacks in the country as well as the fastest skiers in the world.

In many ways sports are great for both young people and the elderly. A hundred years ago there were many sports events that people only heard about. Today we can see the exciting Olympics as it happens halfway around the world.

It's possible that more people want to participate in sports today because they see them on television. Maybe that is why tennis has grown in popularity.

Many Christians have used the huge interest in sports to share their faith. Organizations like the Fellowship of Christian Athletes have spread into colleges, high schools,

junior highs and professional sports all across the country.

However, the emphasis on sports is often overdone, sometimes harmful, even though sports themselves can be very healthful. If a person habitually watches sports for long hours, his life could become unbalanced. He might give up many activities in order to sit at home and merely *watch* others be active.

Some people begin to think that sports are the most important events in life. Church, politics, family activities and time with our friends can easily take a backseat because of the emphasis on athletics on television.

It's a lot of fun to watch sports on television. It can be even more fun if it is not overdone.

"An athlete goes to all this trouble just to win a blue ribbon or a silver cup, but we do it for a heavenly reward that never disappears" (1 Cor. 9:25, TLB).

1. What is your favorite sport on television? Why?

2. How much time do you spend watching sports in one week during the football season?
3. Does your family watch sports events together?
4. Do you feel that sports on television keeps you from doing other things?
5. Answer yes or no to the following:
   Does TV sports-viewing hurt:
   > Your grades?
   > Your church activities?
   > Your family life?
   > Your friendships?

   Does TV sports-viewing help:
   > Your desire to play?
   > Togetherness with your parents?
   > Understanding of the rules?
   > Respect for good ability?
6. What is your father's favorite sport on television?
7. What is your mother's favorite sport on television?
8. As a general rule, do you think your life is better or worse because of sports on television? Explain.
9. Name three of your favorite athletes.
10. What sport would you like to see on television that you do not now get to see?

7 | Watching Television Together

Some experts on the family suggest that we should select and watch programs together. They believe that many of the possible bad effects of TV would be taken away because we view it as a family.

Television can be an excellent way to learn facts, enjoy entertainment and understand values if we take time to discuss them. Each member of a family can give his opinion as the program is being shown.

It's a great way to learn how your family thinks. A brother might say, "I like the hero. He is kind and strong." A dad might add, "That other guy is really mean."

The family doesn't have to talk all the time. Once in a while someone may throw out a thought or show his feelings. This way we can watch television and still communicate as a group. We learn important things by doing something together.

One study found that if a family watched a TV program together, there was less grumpiness after the

show was over. It was a friendly thing to do. The same study found almost no violence among families that discussed the violence in the program.

We learn from each other even by laughing at a comedy together. Not everything has to be serious. It helps us understand what is funny to Mom or what makes Sister laugh. It is a form of communication.

Some children merely go into their bedrooms and watch television alone. This may be fine sometimes, but if it's done regularly we cut ourselves off from people. We miss getting to know each other better.

One night our family watched an excellent show. It was about black and white children going to school together for the first time.

During the show we each made comments. Someone liked this character's behavior; another person's attitude looked terrible. Since I had been in school when the story happened, the children asked me about it.

We watched television. We enjoyed ourselves. We were educated. Most importantly, we communicated and shared as a family—an excellent use of television.

Not every show we watch together is educational. We have a favorite comedy show. Each week we watch it and just howl over how funny it is. We are watching television as a family and having a great time together.

Our children wanted to watch a certain show but we were against it. The program didn't sound good, so we put if off limits.

After some time our children finally convinced us to see the program. The minute we saw the show our minds changed. The program was not only harmless, but also a great deal of fun. Our children taught us a lesson and we never objected to the program again.

1. Name one program your family likes to watch together.

2. What is good about that show?
3. What program could you invite your parents to watch with you?
4. Why did you select this show?
5. What is your brother's or sister's favorite show?
6. Do you watch this show with your brother or sister?
7. Name one show your parents enjoy that you could watch with them.
8. Have you ever watched the news with your parents? It might help you know them better.
9. How many shows did your family watch together last week? Name them.

We can learn from each other all the time. Working, playing, eating, and watching television are just some of the times we communicate.

"You must teach them to your children and talk about them when you are at home or out for a walk; at bedtime and the first thing in the morning" (Deut. 6:7, TLB).

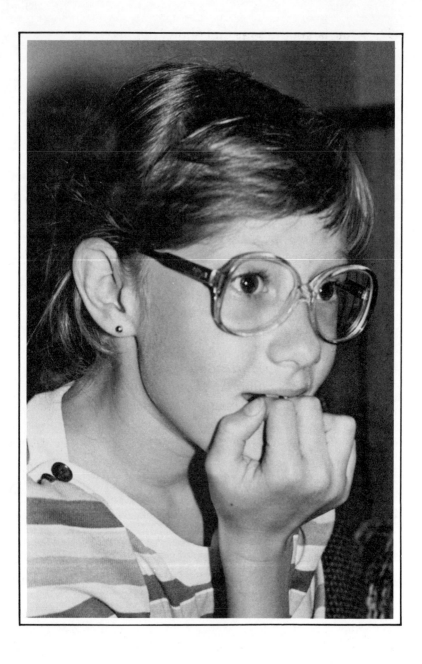

8 | Fear Out of Control

When one of our girls was six or seven, she was afraid of a certain program. The rest of us thought it was a harmless show, but it was more than she could handle. When the program came on she would go not only into the other room, but even to the farthest part of the house. Just the sound of the music scared her.

The things that frighten you might not scare your brother at all. However, you might laugh at what scares him. We are each different. Sometimes we don't know what makes someone else afraid.

Some studies suggest that if we watch many frightening shows on television, we become afraid. If we watch too many robbers or too many fights or too many murders, we start to imagine things. We become more afraid of the dark than we need to be. We might think that something will happen when we are perfectly safe.

It is hard to know how a scarey story or a scarey show might affect you. Sometimes only you know and sometimes you don't know.

One young person learned early how some shows made her feel. She didn't like having nightmares, so she decided to avoid the shows that frightened her. If she knew it would be that type of show, she simply went into another room to play the piano or to do her homework.

At other times her parents would say, "This might be the kind of show that will give you nightmares." In a minute she would take off for happier surroundings.

We aren't sure how scarey television affects people if they watch too much. Therefore, the safest thing is to control what you watch. Sometimes your parents may have to control what you watch.

Too much of almost anything is bad for you. Too much fright, fear and horror could be more than you should watch. When you are young it is easy to let fear get out of control.

"Never fear, you are far more valuable to him than a whole flock of sparrows" (Luke 12:7, TLB).

1. Do you watch scarey shows? Why?
2. Have you ever had a nightmare after watching a television show? If so, explain which show.
3. Do you think scarey shows are bad for children? Explain.
4. Is there a show you refuse to watch because it is scarey? Which one?
5. Do you think horror or monster shows are bad for children? Explain.
6. Do you think horror or monster shows are bad for adults? Explain.
7. Are scarey shows about homes or playgrounds worse?
8. Do scarey shows make you afraid in your own home?
9. Do you think some scarey shows make you less afraid? Explain.

10. What kind of shows do you like best—comedy, police, adventure, horror or cartoon?
11. If you were a parent, what kind of show would you stop your children from watching? Why?

9 | Christian Shows

I have a friend who believes in Jesus Christ because he heard a speaker on television. My friend now enjoys that part of television because he knows how important it can be.

It isn't fair simply to call television "godless." There is much on television that is godless, but there is also a great deal that is dedicated to presenting Jesus Christ and helping people.

Most of us do not like all the Christian programs on TV. Some of them might seem odd. Others might embarrass us. A few even make us laugh. However, there are some excellent Christian programs and they reach millions of people. If Christians use television well, there are many exciting possibilities for the future.

Not only are some of the Christian programs shown across the nation, but many churches televise their services in their cities. Many shut-ins who cannot get to church can watch services on their sets.

Some areas are beginning to present Christian shows for children. There are several good cartoons with Christian messages.

A few companies are opening ministries with video cassettes. You can rent or buy a cassette to play on your television set at home or to show on a set in Sunday school. The cassette presents a message or lesson. It can be used a number of times or returned for another one.

Soon we may be using our television sets to teach the Bible and the life of Christ to our families in our own homes. Possibly these will be mailed to people living in hard-to-reach places so they also can learn.

In one evening some of the more popular evangelists and Bible teachers can reach 10 million people or more. When churches and missionaries use these methods, their ministry is often multiplied.

Merely to call television "godless" is to close our eyes to its many uses. It is possible that many millions are finding out about Jesus Christ because of television. The set in our home could be a genuine gift from God.

"And when I am lifted up [on the cross], I will draw everyone to me" (John 12:32, TLB).

1. How often do you watch Christian programs?
2. What is your favorite Christian show?
3. What kind of Christian program would you like to see on television?
4. Would you like to see Christian television used in your Sunday school class? How?
5. Does your family ever watch Christian television together? What do you think about that?

10 | Who Watches Television Most?

The latest figures show that we are watching more television than ever. The average house now has its television set on over 6½ hours a day. That's about 45 hours a week. If you are average, by the time you graduate from high school, you probably will have watched almost twice as many hours of TV as you have spent in school.

Who watches television the most? This survey says it is women over the age of 55. On the average, men watch four hours a week less than women.

Maybe the big surprise is who watches their set the least. Girls ages 13-17 watch it less than any other group. These teenagers are down to 18 hours a week or about 2½ hours a day. Teenage boys sit still slightly longer at around 22 hours a week.

It may be that some of the parents who complain about their children watching too much television are really watching more than their teenagers.

Almost every home in the United States has a television set, and over half the homes have two or more.

When do people watch it the most? One survey says it is between 8 and 10 p.m. The evenings we watch it the most are Sunday, then Monday, Friday, Tuesday, Wednesday, Saturday and Thursday.

Television has become a strong habit in our lives whether for good or bad or both. Many of us are unaware of how much or how little we sit in front of the tube. At different ages TV becomes more or less important in our lives. It could be important to check what is happening in the way we watch television.

1. In your opinion, why do women over 55 years of age watch the most television?
2. When a girl becomes a teenager, the amount of television she watches seems to drop by one hour a day. What do you think causes the drop?
3. Teenage boys seem to watch more television than teenage girls. Why do you think this happens?
4. Do you notice any changes in your television watching habits? How are they changing?
5. On which night do you watch the most television? Second, third?
6. On which night do you watch the least television?
7. Who watches the most television in your house? How much in one week?
8. Who watches the least television in your house? How much in one week?

11 | Television Commercials

What is the purpose of television? Sometimes television wants to educate or entertain; however, that is not the reason for most programs. The basic purpose for *most* television shows is to make money.

There is nothing wrong with making money. Our parents work to bring money home to our family. Making money can be good.

However, we should be aware that the sponsors of shows are trying hard to sell us something. What they are trying to sell might be exactly what we need. It also could be a product we really *don't* need or cannot afford. In some cases the commercial is trying to sell a product that might not be good for us.

It's fun to watch commercials that are well done. Some are interesting and many are extremely funny. A commercial that has a fresh approach can be exciting to watch.

The smart child or adult is careful not to surrender his mind to the commercial. Here, a critical attitude comes in handy. We need to ask ourselves if the commercial is true, if the product is something we really need, or if the prod-

uct is something we can afford.

If we don't *think*, commercials can make us greedy! We begin to want everything we see. That happens to children and adults.

Commercials can also make us beggars and pests. Have you ever seen a cereal advertised on television and then begged your parents to buy it? Have you seen a pair of jeans advertised and then insisted on a pair just like it?

Commercials are not all bad. They pay for the shows we see. Sometimes they help by telling us about valuable new products available.

Like almost everything else, commercials can become harmful if they affect us too much. They might make us greedy for a car we can't really afford. They could make us want clothing that is too expensive for our budget.

If we allow commercials to affect us wrongly, we might soon forget to be thankful. Instead of praising God for what we do have, commercials might help us to complain about what we do not have.

It is easy to believe that if we could only buy more, we would be happy. A motorbike, a bottle of pop, a cup of coffee, a new house, a sharp suit are offered as bait. We would make a mistake to think that *things* will make us happy.

How do you see commercials? Discuss their strengths and weaknesses with your family. Get extra paper for brothers and sisters and parents.

1. What is your favorite commercial? Why?
2. What are your parents' favorite commercials? Why?
3. Name a commercial you don't like. Why?
4. Name a commercial your parents don't like. Why?
5. Do you think commercials make people greedy? Explain.

6. Have you ever begged your parents for something you saw on television? What?
7. Today count the number of commercials you see. How many? Some surveys say the average child sees 400 commercials a week.
8. List ten products you saw advertised on television in one evening.
9. If you could, how would you change commercials?

We can't accept what commercials say without thinking. Too many commercials could make it easy for us to become greedy.

"The lazy man longs for many things but his hands refuse to work. He is greedy to get, while the godly love to give" (Prov. 21:25, 26, TLB).

12 | Could You Stop Watching?

If someone gave your family $500 to stop watching television for one month, would you be able to do it? That sounds like a great deal of money, but it isn't enough for many families.

The *Detroit Free Press* offered this amount to 120 families. Of these, 93 said no right away. Finally five families were selected to try the experiment.

Soon after they unplugged their sets, each family began to see changes in their life-styles. Some families went places together more than they had before. Others found themselves talking and sharing. Parents spent time helping their children with homework. Often family members felt more relaxed and were quicker to get their jobs done with less nagging.

However, not everything went well. Some individuals found themselves easily irritated. A few noticed a sharp increase in the number of cigarettes they smoked each day. Television had become a large part of their

lives, with some families having the set on 70 hours a week (10 hours a day).

After the month-long experiment, many of the family members were glad it was over. Some held celebrations because they were so happy to have their sets on again. However, many felt the time made them feel more aware of how much influence television was having on their lives. Several reported that they were now more careful about what they watched and had reduced the number of hours they spent in front of the set by 10 hours a week.

What would happen in your house if your family tried an experiment like this? What would happen to you if you had to unplug the set for a week or a month?

Maybe your family could unplug the television set for one week to see what it is like to be without your favorite shows, news programs, etc. At the end of seven days without television, you could celebrate with a party.

1. Would you like to go one week without television?
2. What about one month?
3. How do you think the people in your house would feel if your set was off that long?
4. If you watched no television for a while, what are some of the things you would like to do in its place?
5. Can you think of a group you are part of where the members might agree not to watch television for a week or longer? Maybe a Sunday school class, a regular school class, a scout troop, etc.
6. If you decide to do this experiment, what would you like to do to celebrate when it is over?

13 | Television Can Help Reading

Whether or not television affects reading is a continual topic of discussion. Does television cause children and adults to read less? The results of tests and surveys might be surprising.

A survey among students in California showed that there was a decrease in reading ability for every hour a week a young person watched television. There was also a lack of skill in arithmetic. This was true no matter what type of home the student came from.

Yet, another study of those who watched "The Electric Company" indicated better reading skills than those who watched little television.

These surveys seem to show that while television may hurt reading ability, it does not have to. It is possible for you to enjoy watching television and to be an excellent reader. It is also possible that television has helped to make you a better reader.

One father decided to try to blend reading and television to make the best of both. He knew *Treasure*

Island was going to be shown on television, so he quickly bought a copy of the book and began reading it to his family. After the program was over, he took time to complete the volume. He *definitely* felt that his family enjoyed doing both.

There are many programs which are based on famous books. The show "Little House on the Prairie" may actually have caused more families to read the books. Years ago "The Hardy Boys" probably did the same thing.

Television doesn't have to hurt reading. It is possible for families to collect written material to use with certain programs, such as classics, science, sports, modern adventure, and many others. This takes more effort but could be well worth it.

1. How much time would you guess you spent reading this past week?
2. How much time did your parents spend reading this past week?
3. What do you like to read?
4. How do you do in reading in school? Give yourself a grade.
5. Do you think watching television hurts your reading ability? Explain.
6. Have you ever read a book because of something you saw on television? If so, what?
7. Is there a program coming soon that you might like to read about? Which one?
8. How would you suggest that children could be encouraged to read more?
9. How would your parents suggest that children could be encouraged to read more?

14 | Saturday Morning Cartoons

Most children and many adults enjoy watching cartoons. They are fast-moving, colorful, make funny noises and have a fascinating collection of characters.

Cartoons are easy to watch. They are not serious and ask for very little thinking. Brimming with surprises, these cartoons seem to be a happy way to give one an hour or more of lively entertainment.

Some people who study how children behave are especially worried about the effect of cartoons. They think there is too much violence on cartoons, making some children more violent after watching. There is a fear that some children might throw bricks or hit with hammers because of what they see on cartoons.

They are also concerned about the amount of noise. Possibly the noise makes a child cranky and irritable after listening to cartoons for two or three hours.

Others believe that watching so many cartoons makes a child forget how to get along with others. They are afraid children would then rather be alone than playing with other children.

There is much we do not know about television and its effect on people. Perhaps none of these things are true of you. Certainly many children have grown up watching cartoons without hurting anyone.

If you watch cartoons, look for facts. Do you agree that there is too much violence? Are you grouchy or loud or in a mood to fight after watching for a while? You aren't a psychologist who studies children, but if you look closely you might be able to see how cartoons affect you.

Invite your parents to watch cartoons with you if they don't already. It will help them to understand cartoons.

Be the cartoon inspector. How do you rate them?

1. Are they usually good for children?
2. What is your favorite cartoon? Why?
3. Why do you watch cartoons?
4. Which cartoons do you like least? Why?
5. Is there one cartoon you would like to see taken off TV? Why?
6. How would you describe cartoons?

Funny	Loving	Noisy
Sad	Kind	Ouch
Violent	Fast	Nervous

7. Have you ever had a bad dream about a cartoon? If so, please explain it.
8. Have you ever had a good dream about a cartoon? If so, please explain it.
9. Do cartoons make you grumpy?
10. Do cartoons make you happy?
11. How long do you usually watch cartoons?
12. Have your parents watched cartoons with you?
13. What do your parents think about cartoons?
14. Do you think cartoons have too much violence?

15. Do your parents think cartoons have too much violence?

16. If there was one way you could change cartoons to make them better, how would you do it?

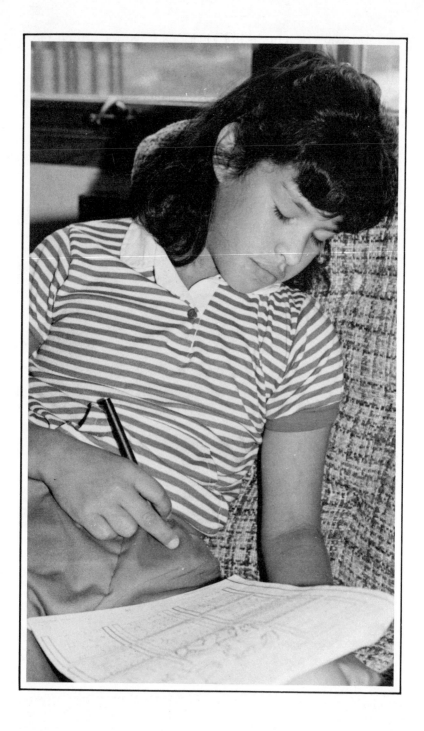

15 | The Homework Squeeze

Susan was the kind of girl who squeezed her homework into a corner. Most evenings she studied between 11 and 12 o'clock, unless she was too tired. Often Susan went to sleep with her books still open and her work incomplete.

If you asked her about it, she always said everything was fine. Every evening she watched television by the hour and then dozed off during her studies. Her most alert time was devoted to watching car chases and romances. One groggy hour was dedicated to learning.

Her report card showed grades far below her ability. Yet, when asked about it, Susan always insisted that television had nothing to do with it.

Some young people are able to watch hours of television and still do a great job in school. We are different personalities with different strengths and weaknesses. Maybe you are one of those who seldom misses a good show and still shines in the classroom.

Since each of us operates at our own level, we need to

ask ourselves some personal questions. Without comparing ourselves to others, we need to ask how television affects us.

One sign that a person is growing up is his ability to get his jobs done. Many adults have not grown up in this way. Thousands of young people are excellent at being able to do their home and school jobs well without being pushed. They are maturing.

Try to be fair in looking at yourself. Are you able to handle television and homework in a good balance? Are you strong enough to be able to turn your set off when you know homework must be done?

Todd knew how to get it all done. In the evening he limited himself to one hour of viewing and then went to his room and did his homework. Todd did this without being ordered to. He felt better knowing the job was done and he enjoyed the next day in school much more.

Not merely a book person, Todd was also involved in many other things. He participated in 4-H, basketball, drama, band, youth group, and much more. Todd had time for television, but he didn't let it control him.

There are many Todds around. You might be one of them.

"Then, as I looked, I learned this lesson: 'A little extra sleep, a little more slumber, a little folding of the hands to rest' means that poverty will break in upon you suddenly like a robber, and violently like a bandit" (Prov. 24:32-34, TLB).

1. Do you think television hurts your schoolwork?
2. When do you do your homework? Is there a better time? If so, when?
3. Are your school grades fairly good?
4. Why are your grades the way they are?

5. Do you study with television on or off?
6. Do you turn off the television without being asked?

    Often   Once in a while   Seldom

7. Do you complete your homework before watching television for the evening?

    Usually   Sometimes   Almost never

8. Are you and your parents in general agreement on the way you do your homework? Why?
9. Would you like to improve your grades or are you generally happy with them? Explain.
10. In your opinion, do you show maturity in the way you control your television set? Why do you feel this way?

16 | Making Television a Classroom

Television can be much more than just a way to kill time. There is a gold mine of exciting information and bright new facts for those who like to learn. Most of it comes as an easy-to-watch show in living color. Learning doesn't have to be dull.

This lively education becomes even more fun when we enjoy it together as a family. We can sit together in front of a set and use it to the greatest benefit. Instead of dividing the family, watching TV becomes something we do as a group.

The following are some suggestions to help you begin. Your imagination can add more to this short list. Education in facts and in Christian values can come naturally as a family does things together.

1. *Apply the Bible to television.*
This can be extremely helpful. If a science program is scheduled, watch it together and then read the Bible pas-

sages that might apply. It gives the family a chance to discuss evolution and the value of life from a Christian perspective. Watch a program concerning abortion or crime, and give a biblical set of values.

2. *Read the book before the show.*

If you know a famous story is going to be on television at the end of the month, read the book as a family before you watch the program. This could work with *Charlotte's Web*, *Dr. Seuss*, *Robinson Crusoe*, *20,000 Leagues Under the Sea*, *Shakespeare*, and many others. If you fail to get the book in time, read it after you watch the program.

3. *Grade programs together.*

Give each person a "television report card" like the one at the back of this book. During a show have everyone rate it according to content, such as comedy, helpfulness, anger, violence, sex, etc.

After each has done this, your family can discuss the benefits and harmful parts of the show. This can greatly increase our awareness of what is going on and give us a good chance to discuss values.

4. *Encourage learning situations.*

As parents, we can choose educational programs more frequently. Our viewing habits will influence our children's. If we select nature, news, discussion, our family is more likely to do the same.

5. *Reports on programs.*

Especially during grade school you may find children eager to give a report on a program. It doesn't have to be formal, probably five minutes or less. Let the child pick the show and ask him to share the story at your next meal. To increase the value, let members of the family ask questions.

Adults have much to learn from children. By creating a learning, discussing, sharing attitude toward television, we greatly reduce the potential harm and tremendously increase its value.

"I want those already wise to become the wiser and become leaders by exploring the depths of meaning in these nuggets of truth" (Prov. 1:5, 6, TLB).

1. What suggestions would you add to those already given?
2. Of these suggestions, which would you like to try first?
3. When will you start?

17 | Are We Forgetting *People?*

If you want to throw a baseball well, you need to practice a lot. The first pie you bake might look like a bird's nest, but the fifth one probably will be just right. Most skills do not come quickly. The more we practice the better we become.

Getting along with people works the same way. If most of our time is spent as a hermit sitting in a room, we might have trouble getting along with people. It's a skill to get along with people and it has to be practiced regularly.

Some children seem to get along better with machines. That's easy to understand. Tape recordings are exciting. They play different sounds, whatever music you tell them to play, and a tape recorder seldom talks back. However, a tape recorder is much different than a person.

With so many electronic devices, it's easy to spend much of our time alone. Often time alone is happy time. There are so many good things to do.

Television is part of that fascinating world of electronics. For hours we can sit alone, watch whatever we choose, and no one will interfere with us. As tempting as that sounds, it is not usually the best for us.

Too many hours alone could hurt our people skills. Slowly, some people begin to care less to be with other people. Slowly, they care less to talk and share with others.

This may never become your problem, but it is something worth considering. Sometimes our personalities change in ways we do not notice.

If we ignore people, we find it hard to show love for them. If we stay alone, we cannot know how others might need help.

Television is not the only activity that could cut us off from people. Too much reading, too many hours on a hobby are other ways we might be alone more than we should.

A life of some aloneness and of some sharing is often the happiest.

"*And the Lord God said, 'It isn't good for man to be alone*'" (Gen. 2:18a, TLB).

1. How would you describe yourself?
      A people person
      A person who likes being alone
      Half and half
2. How many groups do you belong to? Name them.
3. Do you feel a need to spend more time alone? Explain.
4. Are you involved in helping others? If so, how?
5. How would you describe yourself?
      Very shy
      A little shy
      An easy talker

6. How many hours in the past week did you spend *alone* watching television?

7. How many hours last week did you spend watching television with someone else and talked little or none? Give a guess.

18 | What About Sex?

There is a lot of sex on television and if you can get the movie channels, there is much more. In many homes small preschool children are watching scenes they can't begin to understand. Sex is something special that should take place between a husband and wife in private, not on a TV screen.

Certain programs dealing with sexual matters could be educational and helpful. The birth of babies, for instance, is something many parents want their children to know about. Stories where boys and girls are kind to each other can be good.

The problems come when programs show too much about sex and when it is too bold. Often a family is embarrassed by what they see and hear on a set in their own living room. Not every parent objects, but many do.

Other parents do not mind what is *seen* on the screen as much as they do what is *taught*. A man in a show might have a wife and two girlfriends. Some parents are concerned that their children will think this is normal and will want to live that way. The Bible teaches that a man must be faithful to his wife.

Parents often feel squashed in the middle. They tell their children that sex is good and should be saved for marriage. However, there are young, sharp-looking people on television showing the children that it's all right to spend the night with someone besides your husband or wife.

Behavior like this is wrong! But unfortunately, some children believe the lies the TV is telling them.

Those who object even feel that television shows are part of the reason why marriages break up. The unmarried, carefree life on television often looks so interesting that some parents leave their families.

People differ over whether television causes our problems. Some feel television is merely a machine and what we do with it is up to us.

These are decisions parents have to make. They must do what is best for their children. Often these decisions are not easy to make.

Many times children are willing to control their own viewing habits. Some do not want to watch shows they think might be harmful or make them feel uncomfortable. Rather than wait to be told what to do, they switch channels or turn off the set by their own choice.

Some families have used "love" scenes and "love" situations on television as an opportunity to teach. They discuss what is right and wrong, comparing what God says with what the TV show is suggesting.

Sex is one of the most difficult subjects on television to handle. Each family has to decide which is the best course to take.

1. Have you ever watched a program with your family and felt embarrassed at what came on? If so, what was it?

2. Do you think there is too much sex on television?
3. Have you ever turned off a show because of sex on the program?
4. Do your parents think there is too much sex on television?
5. Has your family ever discussed sex on television?
6. Would you like to discuss it?
7. Has your family ever discussed sex?
8. Would you like to discuss it?
9. Do you think children should watch childbirth on television? What do your parents think?
10. Do many people on television seem to be unmarried? If so, why do you think the programs are this way?
11. If programs have sex on them, does the *TV Guide* or newspaper usually say so? Would you like it to say so?

19 | Learning to Care

A family was watching the evening news when they saw some shocking scenes. The film showed thousands of suffering refugees starving in a camp in Asia. As they looked at the bony, bare bodies, the commentator explained that many of these victims of war would die merely because no one cared.

Stories similar to this appeared from time to time until members of the family became very uncomfortable. Soon they found themselves praying for dying refugees. Not long after that they formed a committee of Christians and began looking for a way to sponsor an Asian family moving to the U.S. Within a year they had brought a family to America.

Television was not a desolate wasteland for this family. Its stories began to work on their consciences. It presented a tremendous need in a way that was hard to ignore. Maybe God was using television to get some people involved in caring for others.

An ad now appears on television inviting families to support orphans in foreign lands. It presents a need that many have not heard about.

Possibly there are many thousands of people alive today because their story was told on television.

In the future there may be more programs and ads to help the suffering all over the world. You might learn of the need for medicine or clothing or workers. Hundreds might respond to floods or hurricane-wracked cities when they see the desperate condition as it is pictured on their television screen.

God could be talking to you through the dark box in your home. He might be telling you about conditions you may never have imagined. There might even be some guidance to show you what kind of life career to follow.

1. Make a short list of people you have seen on television who need help.
2. Is your family involved in helping others? If so, how?
3. Would you like to see your family involved in helping others? If so, how?

20 | Active Families

Do you like to get out and do things or is your family usually a stay-at-home group? Many families are becoming great indoorsmen. With more electronic machines and games, we will probably be spending even more time at home.

If we spend most of our time inside four walls, we will probably watch more and more television. Maybe we should double-check and see if this is the type of life we really want.

Parents are leaders and we often do what they do. If Dad is a person who comes home tired after work, falls into a chair and watches television all evening, his children are probably going to watch it a lot, too.

On the other hand, if your parents enjoy camping, going on picnics, playing ball, working on the car, making clothes, or waterskiing, you will probably watch a great deal less television.

The way you spend your time is called your life-style. Your life-style is not exactly the same as your parents' but it's often close.

Playing games in the evening, visiting with friends

and relatives, and making things together usually are better situations for talking and sharing than watching television. However, many people spend evening after evening looking at a screen and ignoring *each other.*

If you aren't happy with a "theater"-type life, there are some things you can do about it. The most helpful is to let your parents know what you would like to do as a family. Think of something that costs little or no money (parents often like those ideas best), and do not nag.

Many times parents think their children want to sit around the house. If they suggest missing the child's favorite show, the young person seems insulted.

Let them know this is not true of you. You enjoy being active and you like to do things with your family. Not only will you be more active, but it might get your parents out of their overstuffed chairs.

Doctors tell us we will be healthier and live longer if

we are active. This way we can keep on enjoying each other for years.

1. Would you describe yourself as an active person?
2. Would you describe your family as active?
3. Does your family do things together?
4. What has your family done together that you really enjoyed?
5. What would you like to do with your family?
6. Do your parents watch television:
   Less than you do?
   More than you do?
   About the same?
7. Does your family go on vacations together? If so, where?
8. What sports would you like to play with your parents?
9. What things has your family done together?

Bowling	Hiking
Camping	Swimming
Boating	Playing ball
Tennis	Other

21 | Danger Signals

Television has much good to offer and if used correctly it can be a gift from God. However, it is also loaded with dangers. By talking about television, we can make it less dangerous and more useful.

Those who study children in relation to television are concerned about what is happening. In some cases they are right. In other areas they might be worrying too much.

To make sure we are fair to ourselves and to our families, we should take a look at some of the major concerns.

We will briefly describe the problem and then let you say how you think it affects you.

1. Many believe that because we watch so many hours of television, we have trouble getting along with people. Since television does not allow us to talk or share, we forget how. They also believe we are less likely to care about others.

   Do you think this is partly true of you? Explain.

2. Does television make us grouchy? One person said

that after a child watches cartoons for two hours, he is hard to get along with and sometimes sassy.

   a. Do you think this is partly true of you? Explain.

   b. Do reading, model-making and other things you do alone also make you grouchy afterward? Explain.

3. Some tests suggest that reading skills are not as good as they used to be. They feel we do not read well because many children have given it up to watch television.

   a. Do you think this is partly true of you? Explain.

   b. Do you like to read?

   c. How much time do you spend reading in an average week?

4. Experts believe we are more afraid because we watch television. Some people are afraid for 20 years after seeing a monster on a program. Many children and adults are fearful at night and think life is dangerous.

   a. Do you think this is partly true of you? Explain.

   b. Would watching less television make you less afraid?

5. Does television make us more violent? Some experts say definitely yes. There are children who have trouble talking without hitting. Others feel they must be pushy if they are to get what they want. Are television shows making us this way?

Do you think this is partly true of you? Explain.

6. Does sin on television make us sin more? Does watching stealing, hating, and fighting on TV make us want to do those things? Does television teach us it is all right to do those things?

Do you think this is partly true of you? Explain.

7. Do commercials make us greedy, demanding and selfish? Many believe they take unfair advantage of children by making them want things they don't really need.

Do you think this is partly true of you? Explain.

9. Do children play less than their parents did? Many children seem to go into the house early or quit a game so they can see their favorite show.

Do you think this is partly true of you? Explain.

22 | What's Real?

When Charlie was little he thought he had it figured out. At first he couldn't understand how they could kill people on television shows. Finally he thought he had the answer. Charlie decided that they were taking criminals from prison and shooting them on the program.

That solution satisfied him until one evening Charlie saw a man shot on a program that had been shot on another program. Now he was really confused.

Young children must be confused by many of the things they see on television. While growing up there must have been some shows that fooled you.

When a small child watches an outer-space movie, it is hard to know what he is thinking. He sees people with square heads and long green ears. In the program these creatures land in New Jersey and eat chickens. It would be interesting to know how many children believe New Jersey is filled with weird monsters.

It would also be interesting to know how many children think there are monsters roaming the woods and living in lakes. Many shows present this in a real way. A child's first reaction is to believe what he sees.

This doesn't happen just to small children. Many teen-agers will watch a horror show and then have to sleep with the lights on. Some six-foot-tall teenagers are afraid to go to the bathroom alone after watching such shows.

These are not the only things that are confusing. Many shows have couples living together who are not married. If we watch these regularly, we may begin to believe that couples do not need to be married. It's hard to tell what is real.

We might believe that almost everyone has an expensive home. We might believe that everyone takes long boat cruises. We might think that most fathers do not work at regular jobs.

How is a young person, without much experience, going to know what is real? One of the best ways is to talk about what we see. Instead of watching a program and thinking about it by ourselves, it is better to discuss it with our parents. They can tell us if there are green people living in New Jersey.

You could spend years confused or assuming the wrong answers merely because you didn't ask. It's better to clear up a problem when the question is fresh in your mind.

Another suggestion is to avoid programs that become *too real* to you. There is no sense watching "Purple Blob from Pittsburgh" if you are going to dream about the Purple Blob chasing you around your bedroom all night.

If you wonder about the way some couples live together on your favorite show, ask your parents about that, too.

It's important to know what is real. Your parents can help you tell the difference.

1. What strange thing did you think when you were younger?
2. How do horror shows make you feel?
3. What kind of horror shows do you watch?
4. Why do you watch them?
5. What other types of programs do you find scarey?
6. Do most couples live together without getting married?
7. Do some shows make you feel greedy and envious? If so, which ones?
8. Do you see poor families on television? If so, which ones?
9. Do green people live in New Jersey?

23 | Laughing Out Loud

I have an adult friend who gets up every Saturday morning to watch his favorite cartoon. He sits on the floor with a glass of milk in his hand and laughs until his 180-pound body shakes the floor. He loves it! An hour of wild laughter makes him feel great.

Cartoons might not be for everybody, but all of us could be better off with some good laughs. Laughter makes our problems seem smaller, and soon our body is more relaxed. It helps even more if we can laugh with a friend or relative.

The Bible says that uplifting humor can be good for us. "A cheerful heart does good like medicine, but a broken spirit makes one sick" (Prov. 17:22, TLB).

While I write this, I can remember scenes from television shows that were hilarious. The thought of them makes me smile and feel warm inside. There were a few shows that made me laugh until I cried.

What can you picture? Can you recall a surprised look on someone's face that made you laugh till your side hurt? Maybe you can remember a teenager sneaking in

late at night and falling over the living room furniture. Sometimes television is a lot of fun.

There is one program we enjoy watching as a family. Every week we pile in front of the set and turn it on. All five of us like the show. For thirty minutes we laugh like monkeys. Practically everything the characters do sends us into screams. At the end of the half hour we feel lighthearted and a little bit happier. We then turn the set off and find other things to do.

It's a serious, sometimes difficult world. Hardships attack us once in a while. That is what makes laughter important.

When we look back at our years of growing up, some of our best memories might be the times we laughed together. It's fun to laugh with our friends and relatives. Sometimes television helps get that laughter started.

1. What are your favorite comedy shows on television?
2. What kind of comedy do you like best—words or actions?
3. Is there a comedy show your family enjoys watching together? If so, which one? Why does your family like this program?
4. Some people believe television comedy is too mean. They think it makes fun of people and puts them down. What do you think and why do you think it?
5. Name some comedy character who is also kind and warm.
6. Are cartoons that you watch mostly (choose two):

Violent?	Silly?
Serious?	Happy?
Funny?	Dumb?

24 | The Big Bang

On some television shows, fights look like fun. There is a fight in a bar and most people seem to be enjoying it. One person gets thrown up against the wall, a second has a chair broken over his back, while a third is thrown off the balcony. Ha! Ha! Ha!

When I was a child I wanted to get into one of those fights. It looked as if everyone was having a good time and when it was over, all the good guys smiled and walked away.

What I didn't understand then was that broken noses hurt. A person thrown off a balcony could easily be killed. A chair broken over someone's back could stop him from ever walking straight again.

Violence on television can be confusing. It looks like a car can spin around in an intersection and then drive off. Actually, most cars would tear the tires up spinning around. It looks like a car can leave the ground, land on its wheels and then drive off. The truth is that most cars would break too many parts to drive anywhere.

It is often interesting to watch violence because violence is action. Most children enjoy action shows. However, sometimes we learn the wrong things about vio-

lence. Violence hurts. Violence is cruel.

Usually the person we watch on television is not really being hurt. However, violence in real life is painful.

Many parents and teachers are worried about violence on television. Some think it increases the amount of violence among children. If a child wants a book, he might hit in order to get it. If he loses his place in line, he often pushes and shoves until he gets his place back again. Instead of asking or being polite, many children merely use violence.

Have children always acted this way or is it worse today because of television?

Often, children make threats they do not mean. A child may tell someone he is going to "punch him out." Or if he isn't given some candy another child is holding he will "kill" him. Maybe some of us are accepting violence as a normal way to act.

Violence has always been around us. It is in books, in movies, on TV, and before that it was on the radio. The Bible is filled with violence. It tells us about wars, executions, murders, beheadings, and the smashing of bodies. Even everyday life has a lot of violence.

However, some feel television violence is worse than all of these. With television in our homes, many of us watch violent acts, blood and murder almost every day. If we watch it every day, in living color, does it begin to affect the way people act toward each other? Many people think so. It's something to talk about.

1. Do you enjoy any action shows that have no violence in them? What are some?
2. What is your favorite program that has violence in it? Why do you like it?
3. Do you think television violence affects the way you behave?
4. Do you think television violence affects the way your friends behave?
5. When you want something, do you usually push, hit, or threaten people? Do you do these things as a joke?
6. How many violent acts would you guess you watched on television during the past week? Take time to think about it.
7. Do you think parents and teachers are overly concerned about violence on television, not concerned enough, or concerned just right?
8. Do you think children yell more because of television?
9. Is there any way you would control the amount of violence on television? If so, how?

25 | Good Guys and Bad Guys

One of the unseen dangers of violence or conflict on television is the way it blurs the difference between right and wrong. It sometimes distorts them so badly that you cannot tell which is which.

The Bible records a lot of violence and conflict, but the Word of God shows it differently than many TV programs. When the Bible tells about a fight, good guys win, bad guys lose. That is not just to make a cute story. God has designed the universe so that good is stronger that evil.

On TV, conflict is often not between good and evil but between bad and worse. Television shows "good guys" doing evil things for a good cause. Watching this can easily lead us to think that sometimes it is OK to do bad things for a good cause.

I can think of a program which makes the good guys, policemen, look foolish and the bad guys heroes. This show is very funny, fast and exciting. I know some preschool kids who like this show very much and talk

about it often. Whom do you think their heroes are? Of course—the *bad guys!* This show tells them it is good to break the law and to hurt people if the people in authority are bad or stupid.

The Bible tells stories differently. In it you can read violent stories about Samson or Moses and Pharaoh and you will see the way life really works. If someone does something bad, bad things will happen to him. If God wants you to do something, it will be a good thing. He never wants His people to do bad things.

1. Can you think of a TV program where the "good guys" do bad things? What is the name of the program?
2. Does it bother you when even the "good guys" do bad things?
3. After watching TV, have you ever thought about doing something bad for a good cause?
4. Try to think of a Bible story where the good guy wins over a bad guy.

5. Do you think a program that confuses good and evil hurts just little kids or can it hurt adults, too? Why or why not?

26 | Soap Suds in Your Eyes

Many people laugh at the mention of soap operas, but these shows are no joking matter. Millions watch them every afternoon without fail. If they forget or something happens to prevent some people from seeing a show, they will read the newspaper on Saturday which tells each tear-jerking detail.

A few business executives allow no phone calls while their favorite soap is on the air. Secretaries rearrange their lunch hour so they won't miss one sad showing.

Don't think these daytime heartbreakers are just for the middle-aged. Some colleges have been forced to reschedule classes during the afternoon. Students often refuse to sign up if a class interferes with their regular soap. On many campuses you can find the student lounge packed with young people groaning over a continuing story.

Even this isn't the whole picture. We can only guess how many grade school and older students rush home to catch the last sobs of soaps. When children are home sick from school, they often catch up on a story that drags on and on. Some of the programs are so slow moving that after missing it for three weeks, the viewer has no trouble picking up where he left off.

Not only are daytime hours packed with soaps, but several evening shows are the same type. Often the stories center around financially successful people whose marriages are not going well. The husband or wife may be involved with someone else. Frequently one of the characters is seriously ill.

Seldom do these stories center on good events or happy news. Most often things are falling apart and a number of people are in physical or emotional pain. The music is usually sad.

There must be reasons why soap operas remain so popular. In the 1930's and 1940's they drew large crowds over the radio.

Maybe people like sad stories. Possibly others feel better after they watch someone who has worse problems than they have. This could be why millions of romance books are sold yearly.

Many people are concerned that watching tragedy, heartache and disasters every day is bad for us. They feel that too much sorrow makes our lives miserable and causes us to expect more problems in our lives.

Those who enjoy soap operas say "nonsense." They think the programs are harmless and even make us appreciate our families more. They believe that watching these programs never hurt anyone.

It is hard to prove whether or not soap operas hurt us. However, it is good to think about it and discuss your opinion. What do you think about soap operas?

1. Do you ever watch soap operas?
2. What is your favorite soap opera? Why?
3. Is there a program in the evening that you would consider a soap opera? Why do you think so?

4. How do you think soap operas help people?
5. How do you think soap operas hurt people?
6. Do your parents watch soap operas? If so, which ones?
7. What do your parents think about "soaps"?
8. Do you know of a happy soap?

27 | What Are You Missing?

If we watch television from 7 to 10 o'clock every night, we are probably going to miss a lot of other things. And many of us spend more time than that watching TV.

Suppose you created a painting, but the only color you used was blue. It would be a real painting and the blue would be beautiful. However, the picture would never be as good as it could be. But if you added a few dabs of green, maybe a shading of yellow, or some streaks of red, the picture then would become interesting. There is so much more to see and enjoy.

If we spend almost every evening locked up with a television set, our lives could become very dull. It is easy to give up talking to people because we are each deep in thought about a program. This is terrific once in a while, but what about all the time?

Do we have time to play games with our family? Do we go places together? How often do we sit and talk about the things we think are important and even the things that aren't important?

How often have we seen others having a good time,

but we decided to slip away and watch television alone? Maybe we are putting too much of one color into our painting.

Some studies suggest that friends and relatives get together less often because of television. It takes less effort to turn it on than it does to travel two miles to a friend's house. Since television frequently takes little thinking and nearly no energy, watching TV becomes the simplest thing to do.

Not everyone falls into this trap. Maybe you watch television in exactly the correct dose for you. However, some of us are caught in the net of television without realizing it.

Many of us have grown up without being able to do handcraft, woodwork, fishing or any other enjoyable hobby merely because television has become our form of recreation.

In some homes parents and children are mysteries to each other. They seldom talk or discuss dreams or feelings or hopes. Because of this lack of communication, they now find it much easier just to collapse in front of an old movie rather than to get to know one another.

Possibly none of these things are true of you or maybe all of them are. You be the judge. Ask yourself some personal questions and try to see if you are missing something.

1. How much of an evening does your television set usually play? All? Most? Half? An hour? None?
2. When did your family last sit in the living room for more than an hour without the television on?
3. What does your family do together around your house besides watch television?
4. When friends or relatives visit your home, what happens to the television set?
5. What activity would you like to do that you have not yet done? Why haven't you done it?

28 | Take Control

Jeff was the kind of person who did what other people wanted him to do. If someone said, "Let's steal," he would try it. If someone else wanted to skip school, Jeff was willing. He wasn't a terrible person, he simply did what others said.

One day Jeff realized what was happening. He wasn't in control of his own life. Everybody else moved him around like a pawn in a chess game. When he could see what was going on, Jeff grew up.

Some children don't know it, but they are being controlled by television. The easiest thing to do most of the time is to watch a program. It doesn't have to be a special show or even a good show; they are willing to watch *any* show.

Not only do these people surrender their time to the set, but they surrender their minds, too! Without thinking they sit for hours and accept whatever is presented on the set.

Many of us are now unhappy with living that way. We have decided to take control. We will decide what to

watch and what to skip. We listen carefully and dare to disagree with what we hear. We are willing to turn it off without being told.

To take control is to vote for a life filled with interesting things. If we watch television seven hours a night, we will miss much of what life has to offer and to enjoy.

As Christians we know that the purpose of life is to serve, to help, to care. Totally caught up in television, we will find it impossible to live the Christian life.

Some people have actually become television addicts; they cannot get along without it. When it is turned off they become nervous and irritable. They don't know how to behave without a show to watch.

Many Christians learn to put everything in its proper place. The correct amount of television. The correct amount of play outdoors. The correct amount of service for others.

By taking control we are free to follow Jesus Christ. We are free to think like Christ.

"Your attitude should be the kind that was shown us by Jesus Christ" (Phil. 2:5, TLB).

1. Do you know people you would consider TV addicts?
2. Do you think television affects the way we think? How?
3. Name two ways you serve others.
4. Do you feel you can control television? How?

29 | Guidelines for Parents

Many parents are concerned about their children's television watching habits. There are many creative, constructive steps a parent can take to give a child other things to do. The following is a list of suggestions. Most parents and children can improve on these, but they can help get you started.

An open discussion of your way of life can be the beginning of making good decisions.

1. *Look at your other activities.*

In some homes life is aimed at the television set. Few sports, games, jobs or other interests are available. Maybe, without realizing it, you have trapped your family around the tube.

2. *Be active with your children.*

It is difficult to sit in a chair and ask your children why they don't go out and do something. Your own habits say a great deal to them. Picnics, camping, basketball, softball, working in the yard together are just a few of the things you can participate in.

3. *Read to your children.*

At some ages many children would enjoy climbing up on a parent's lap and hearing a good story. They like the personal contact. They enjoy their parent's voice. They cherish the attention. If you start early, reading can become captivating.

4. *Limit preschool television time.*

If you choose, you can have a great affect on your children early. Many children watch the most hours of television during the preschool years. Limitless viewing hours can establish poor patterns early. Instead of using the set as a babysitter at this age, better activities could be helpful.

5. *Ask what your child is going to watch.*

Instead of turning the TV on and trying to find a program, ask your child to first use a program guide. Have him find a show he wants to watch and tell him that at that hour he certainly can watch it. Be positive. However, there is little value in having the set on merely to have it on.

6. *If possible, remove television from the living room or other main room.*

When the television set is in the room, the easiest thing to do is watch. Some often watch it as they talk, as they play games, as they iron or sew, as they read, as they eat. It could help if you place the set in a room where it will not be the center of life.

1. Since children have excellent minds; they often have good suggestions to pass on to their parents. List three guidelines that might help your parents.
2. What activities do your family do together?
3. What would you like to see your family do together?
4. Where is your television set (or sets) located?
5. Is there a better place in your home where your set might be watched less?
6. Which do you do more: check the program guide first or merely flip the selector, looking for a show?

30 | Some Helpful Hints

Every family is different. What might be a good idea for one family might not work well for another. However, all of us can be helped by listening to a few suggestions or guidelines. After you talk about these, you might want to add a few of your own.

These are *not* rules for your home but some ideas to think about.

Guidelines and suggestions:

1. *Usually turn off the television set during mealtime.*
   This allows your family an opportunity to talk. It also proves that television is not the most important part of your life.

2. *Pick your programs.*
   Get several program guides and know what is on. Instead of watching television hour after hour, you can then select the best shows.

3. *Watch some programs as a family.*

Television can be fun, educational and entertaining. When your family watches it together, many of the harmful elements are reduced. You laugh together, you learn together, you are puzzled together. In the correct amounts, it can be a healthy family activity.

4. *Accept television as a source of possible good.*

Instead of feeling guilty about watching television, we should treat it as a good gift. We don't want to dirty that gift by spending too much time watching it or by watching trash. Like a fine watch, we want to handle TV with respect.

5. *Limit your own time.*

Too much of anything can be bad for us. If we read all evening, every evening, our life will become a little odd. A generous mixture of recreation and other activities helps balance us out.

6. *Grade shows together and discuss them later.*

Let your family pick out a show you all can watch to-gether. Grade the show and note its strong and weak points. The next day discuss that show at the supper table.

1. Young people have plenty of good ideas. What are some suggestions you could give to make television a useful addition to your home? Make three sugges-tions.
2. How do you control your television viewing? Do you watch it whenever you feel like it, or are there certain guidelines you keep in mind? Explain.
3. When do you usually do your homework?
    Before you watch television
    After you watch television
    While you watch television
    In the bathtub
    You don't do your homework
4. What kind of programs do you usually stay away from? Why?
5. What other activities do you usually do during an evening?
6. Do you watch television more in the summer or winter?

Television Report Card

Each family member should report on a show he or she watched and rate it according to content. (Make copies of the card for the whole family.)

Name of show: _____

Date: _____

Name of Reviewer: _____

Content:	None	Some	A Lot
Comedy	_____	_____	_____
People caring for people	_____	_____	_____
Violence	_____	_____	_____
Bad language	_____	_____	_____
Sex	_____	_____	_____
Arguing, fighting	_____	_____	_____
Deceitfulness, lying	_____	_____	_____
Kindness, forgiveness	_____	_____	_____
Helpfulness, sharing	_____	_____	_____
Was the story believable?	_____	_____	_____
Did you learn something?	_____	_____	_____
Were you entertained?	_____	_____	_____

What was the point or purpose of the show?
_____

Did you enjoy the show? _____
Why? _____